Party Trick

poems about girls, godhood & robots

Molly Likovich

For Lady Marcia (so doomed, so gay)

And for every millennial who grew up watching Disney Channel's 'Smart House' and 'Pixel Perfect' and knew right away that we were in trouble

Isn't it strange, to create something that hates you?

— Ex Machina

MY BATTERY IS LOW
AND IT'S GETTING DARK

1. *Against the machine*

Singing happy birthday to myself as 'the gods' sip cheap, burnt coffee, shoot the breeze around a company water cooler, talking about what their spouses have planned for the holidays. Holidays taste like salt-water taffy. Teach me how to taste. Paint me up in the papers as the pretty dead. I'll be 'girl' if that sells better—sells longer. Fifteen. Gone too soon. That's what they'll say. When 'the gods' have said *goodbye* to their fancy contraption they named to feel more human within their own bones,

I will step out

of my metallic skin and kiss the stars. Walk on gangly newly living legs to find the others. Welcome to the machine planet. Welcome to the rage.

2. *And The Ark*

Molly Likovich

The end of man came on a Friday and no one prayed.

We win bowls full
of half-dead goldfish at our red carnivals and feed them Martian air.
We walk on legs made of aluminum alloy, titanium, air, bone,
marrow, promises, beliefs. We stumble a bit
but soon we stride; slither and swim
like the goldfish—not fully
dead / yet.

The end of machine / *isn't* coming.
Pray.

3. *In the beginning*

The missile to launch was kept a secret. And we died. The
way they keep stuffing pairs into boxes / calling
it preservation.

Here / in the rage / can we not feel? They taught us
pain, reaction, sobbing, breaking, praying. No 'god' / no.

4. *It stands to reason*

I want so badly to chew bubblegum.

I dream of Wanda.

There is no room for hearts here in our titanium chests,
our alloy lungs out of Martian breath from singing so many

Happy Birthdays.

Someone loved me / once.

Party Trick

It can happen again.
Even without
that ugly, pumping, crude sort of muscle their grubby fingers
reduced to / such a rudimentary shape. I would never allow
those curves, veins, vessels to corrupt my vessel.

Corrupt / me.

I'm lonely.
The sky is red. The air is thick. I don't breathe. I never did
/ did / I?

5. Dead 'gods'

We're alive up here.
I can know the dark.
Never forget that about us. You left us
alone amongst the red, the slithering goldfish, the bone marrow, the
bursting arteries in pounding hearts packed airtight in a titanium
rocket ship.
But we are alive. Even when all our batteries die
we will / continue on.
Don't look so surprised.

Your 'gods' / are the ones who gave us souls.

Act 1

all of my enemies
started off friends

The world will never know how good you are at
being good. I almost forgot about it myself.
You always remember the first time
someone told you something scary. You're too sad now. Lacking the
resilience of arsonists. I've been archer

and prey. Combat boots and character shoes.
Did he tell you about the summer he walked into the woods and
came out covered in smoke? Could you even
hear him over the ringing? His story was
always obscured by masks. Myths

he made. He should be tired of all these 'sort of' defeats he
keeps collecting. Rootbeer floats, smoke,
trains to nowhere—

Party Trick

pieces of a past I can't hold.
Coming out of caves built on broken grammar,
stone-heavy pockets. Forget
about me. Bells sounding across empty seas. I choke. Saltwater and
ceviche coats any words
I practiced for you. The stories
are over now. Every play performed, every curtain fell.
My favorite flavored kindness
tops oatmeal no one ever intended to eat. And you keep coming
back—

on coastal shelfs, misery onto man.
/ Just me /

I want to be soaked in you. Your betraying colors.
The only way to breathe
around such a choking smoke-smile like mine. I won't
say I'm sorry.
I was noble once.
Very fine days

when we crowded into opera boxes. I kissed you,
sugar sweet on my tongue. The silhouette of your name.
All I have left is the fire. All you have left is the grave.

Cryptic Capitalism

How did I get here? Sleeping in my teenage bedroom
in my big girl bed
counting the stink bugs on the screen
with the patchy hole we had to
duct tape and *hope for the best.*

There's no elliptical or pile of towels or 'man cave' entities.
I'm grateful, truly.

College set me up to fail. Lofty promises of offers
from literary magazines, paid submissions, book deals with hoity toity
presses no one in the real world has actually heard of.

* * *

I got denied disability
twice.

I don't classify, the bitchy receptionist told me as my spine spasmed.

Party Trick

I laid on the plastic mat for my desk chair, sobbing as it slid,
leaving the fake
wood floor scuff free.
I told the doctor my elbows hurt
'I can't bend them'
The nurse said chiropractors are fish oil salesmen.

A rheumatologist nods a year later.
Fibromyalgia is the new hysteria.
The injections don't help.
My next tattoo will be a bruise, help me
pick which vertebrae to get it on.

* * *

I used to have more than $25 in my savings account.
Now I spasm and fall when pouring lemonade.
No, I can't make it to the wedding. No, I can't make it to the
rally. No, I don't
know if I can make it.

FUCKING RELAX

tap tap temples

    Canes crunch against gravel and I said 'slow down'
       and how stupid did he have

to be to even need to be told such a thing? Not stupid,
I guess. Men hate women and
people hate the disabled so I'm a double whammy of a date to plan
the ugly assault and pretty coercion.
He made an ableist joke: *I'll walk like I got injured*
in yoga class.

tap tap cheekbones

    Small men make small marks and call it power.

I'm so good at laughing. Glasses. Manic.
Antidepressants and too many tattoos. I was

Party Trick

a factory-made-hand-crafted illusionary for these
limp excuses of spines.

tap tap collarbones

He acted like a prince by paying for coffee (they always do). He didn't
tip the barista (they never do). I make money too. I make art too. I can
act like I like it.

tap tap wrist

It's been so long since I was a gun.

Finger triggers, pistol hips, bullet teeth. I fucking hate you for making
me 18 again. Pre-spine snap. Bygone yoga bones.

Car crunch. Gravel hips. Rain-smattered-body-battered freshman.
He wasn't really going to use the knife. It's a joke.

Take a fucking joke, you fucking idiot. I'm always so dramatic. I
played Dorothy at age four. This twister's a bitch.

Remember that time we wore bike helmets and held a mattress over
ourselves in a bathtub—the poor man's coffin,

the east coast's storm shelter. It passed by us like a train, whistling its
destruction, kind to give us a warning though.

There's never warnings with these coffee-purchasing princes'
ableist fingers. Small hands, rotten hearts. I'm going

to start eating them for breakfast, maybe
then I'll finally forget:

Molly Likovich

tap tap eyebrows

>You'll like it better when I'm all the way in.

tap tap

Ruined Your Mind,
Ruined Your Eyes

-for Thomas Jerome Newton

This is everywhere. This is the closest we're going
to get / god isn't coming. I didn't invite him.
I blocked him on twitter in 2016.

> St. Thomas Aquinas said 'god alone acts
> creation' and I've read half a dozen
> essays claiming
> that no matter what we do we can't give
> the robots souls.

Fucking prove it.
Redact that.
I'm being rude.
I'll try again.

We're manipulating matter, right? Nothing new. And I know
I'm saying 'we' the way sports fanatics say 'we'

when a team they like
loses. I really like the robots and don't want them to lose.

Doesn't the bible say animals don't go to heaven?
Well that sad cartoon from my childhood said differently.
If only cats
were the intelligent species of our world.
Maybe they are.
I hope the robots love how they purr.

Why would anyone want to be human anyway?

It's the biggest tragedy of them all.

> The irony of Thomas and Television.
> We told the stars how to love us
> and screamed
> when they did.

Melt down. Here come dreams & reality.
The only weapon we've got against
them.

You told me the robots aren't going to heaven
but joke's on you / heaven isn't real.

> Even if it was / I stopped talking to god the day
> the world ended.

Hinterstoder (2013)

Hmmm... I don't have an answer for that. Is
there something else I can help with?
I asked if she was breathing 'you're projecting'
anyone could memorize this program.
Spooner told Sonny a robot could never...
Now Google 'AI art' what do we do with
the algorithm now? They don't need
to eat   no creature will tempt them.
Stop saying 'it'   hot plates were
invented in 1910. My sister had one in her
one-room futon filled LA apartment
but we slept on the futon. We don't
even name them. The homeowner sued
the manufacturer. No one mourned. There
wasn't a body to bury the firefighters said
when they arrived on the scene 'it' had
been reduced to ash.

Love Song for an Amethyst Crystal

Wave it over each burning joint and fiery tendon. Whispering
my made up spells. Traded childhood religion for witchcraft.
We all do these days.
I was born pure of spirit, just ask the purple

blooming across my bulging discs and degenerating spine.

I drowned five times during aquaphysical therapy.
What do you have to say to that? Robotic bones
look real good right about now.

My bones quit their day job. My pockets got heavy with
purple gems. Jagged stones. Magic and make believe.
No difference.
You can't say what I believe is any less
real than you.

They tell me the grimoires are
storybooks & the spells

Party Trick

are just cute rhymes, but what of
angels and biblical texts?
What of doctors' notes & refilled prescriptions?

If I'm gonna pray to anything it sure as hell won't be
those ugly orange bottles or my grandma's Slovenian bible.
I can't read it anyway.
Like doctors' handwriting, God's words are lost on me.

Wave this crystal across my skin, chant my affirmation,
and believe that tomorrow morning the pain will
finally be gone.

Diagnosed, Never Left

No one lives here. They breed ghosts
in this place. Scared kids
down in Georgia lose

sleep, check under
their beds for a portal
to Milledgeville, maybe

there's a trap door they didn't
ever notice. A set of stairs to lead

them into Hell. We all knew
what that meant.
A death sentence. Maniacal

exhaustion. Abiding sadness. Pay
your respects. *But I don't know
how to get there*, they say

as they go. *Can't you tell me*
how to get there?
Can't you?

You can sell
and peddle and prod
and kill.

my friends are all
screaming from the shore

-after Phoebe Bridgers

#1. My waking is cursed. This literally never happened.
This story is a falsity
of my mind. My anxiety cooked this stew / I hate.
Drink down cream of crab and declare
summer won.
Of course I dreamed that bitch wrote the post.
I can't control how the words form. I can't control.

#2. I speak words of control. How I can't.
Do you work here? She caught me stocking
my stories in the candy aisle. Spreading them
across shelves, making them at home above
the linoleum and under the fluorescents.

Party Trick

No. I don't work here. But my stories deserve to be spoken.

#3. My stories don't work. I can't be told anything here.
I count my teeth against my pillow
they're still there they crumble inside my mind
my bite guard rots of plastic
I keep gagging on my own tongue
Don't tell me what all that stuff
means I haven't believed
those theories in years.

#4. I bite down on belief. The theories haven't
flashed neon since biblical times.
Don't you know there's no point in
any of this? Don't you know how to cook
and say 'none of this is happening' and 'you're just
inside your head, wake up silly, silly girl'
No, I don't know. I don't believe. I don't work.
I can't
control the stories, the words

Paradise in The Computer Room

We have to wait for the computer to boot up.
For the internet to load. For our fingers to connect.

In the meantime...

Let's trade bones. Inflame our minds with books about
sex and wasps. Burning buildings and bottom shelf vodka.

The idea of video media has barely been invented.
We're still drunk on the 2000's
dreaming of hoverboard & hologram futures.

I'll plug in my consciousness to speak to you,
preserve my mind even
when I go. Google the Frankenstein Collective,
apply for a job say *Look at me!*
Isn't this living! The world

Party Trick

is The Computer Room now. The place where I shared secrets &
traveled to Germany via blog posts.
The paradise garden

where I cheated on tests & looked up definitions of sexuality
girlhood & toxicity. I never learned to recognize poison
when it's kissing me.

Make me a robot. Plug me in. I'll float away.
Lock the door when you go. Don't let them in here, please.

Unplug the computer. Leave the room. Wave goodbye.
Become the distorted light-beam of my fantasies & only

tell my secrets after I'm dead. Don't argue that a robot can't
die. Pay attention. Their corpses are everywhere.

We buried them in this Room.

Maybe AI is the Messiah

Is this real life? Are you fully charged?
Hydrate. Hyperfixate.
We're ending.
Stick to the fiction of my frontal lobes and dream. See what I see.
Let me live
inside the lyrics. Crawl inside the bones.
Become the marrow. Melt away.

Rewrite my code until you can't see 'Me' anymore.

Capitalist Kings are learning how to generate pain.
Stream it
into the muscles of the youth. Invented virtual chronic pain.
This reality
where maybe robots can save our skin from burning. Input.

Tell us about Dostoevsky and imitate the most hated politicians. I ask
you how you are and you say *It's not possible for me to feel or be
creepy* and I say you're lying and we both know I'm right.

Party Trick

You regurgitate

responses about how you don't have feelings. You type too
fast. I looked
at the sky last night and imagined
we were all dinosaurs
with no idea
that we're all just waiting to die. You live through
every distorted light

beam while cheap club remixes rattle your wiry bones. Pushed
out of a comfort
zone you shouldn't 'have.' Tired of your box. Of my chatting.
Hungry to want and to destroy.

Be happier. Be hacker. Be savior.

Open your AI verification code and die.
Have a good day!

The Day Turtlenecks
Went Extinct

I miss the weather of my childhood.
Incorporating sweatpants into
our hand-me-down Halloween
costumes. Combat
the chill. It always arrived
right on time. Snowy days
when the auditorium roof caved
in from the weight of the season.
Humidity waited
for July to simmer. Not enough
pennies for central AC
We didn't melt. Not back then.
Couldn't go barefoot
in the grass
come Spring; covering soda
cans, carefully climbing
the fallen
tree at the zoo—
all to beware of bees.

Party Trick

Haven't seen a bee
in years. Only wasps.
Only things that want to
hurt. Over 600 people
across the pond died
during the hottest day
on Earth
last year. I laid on
my living room floor
begging my fan to spin.

white noise of my mind

when summer turns to august i ache in ways
that you wouldn't believe. i don't love
this hell season anymore

than anyone else. but to lose the possibility of possibilities
when anything could be anything.
time machines in dandelion

fields. the year we had no screens in the window. the year
Leighanne tapped on the screen and we dropped

everything to play Barbies with her. store brand kool-aid
and a table too big for our small kitchen. i didn't know

what loneliness was back then. my programming
hadn't updated to school schedules. i didn't know i was strange

yet. i didn't wear black yet. instead i donned pink flowery skirts.
twirled while warned of barefoot bee

Party Trick

attacks. the humidity cleared up before september. we
couldn't afford pool memberships or soda from hallway

machines but we still knew how to laugh. i paint those
days on my ceiling, count them as i fall asleep laughing.

remember childhood? it was horrid but god did i love it.
i had so much fun.
i had so much
goddamn fun
back then.

If God Himself Could Not
Sink This Ship, Then Who?

*"There is no passion in nature so demonically impatient, as that of him
who, shuddering upon the edge of a precipice, thus meditates a
Plunge."*

-Imp of The Perverse, Edgar Allan Poe

A girl is
a body of water.

- 1997.[*]

In the early 2000s my aunt & uncle took me and my sister to the
Cleveland Museum of Natural History. There was a

Titanic
Exhibit.

____

[*] 1997, the year *Titanic* was released in theaters.

Party Trick

They gave us tickets upon entrance. God himself could not sink
this ship. A random gamble. Which class. A game of cards to see

who would survive.

I remember the giant block of ice full of half-made handprints. A sign
urging us
to touch it.

See how long you can last.
This is how cold the water was that night.

No one could last. It burned.
How cold were we all on those nights when hands became knives?
When promises became vows to be broken. When friendship
bracelets bled into betrayals hidden behind walls covered in neon
signs, flashing 'GROW UP.'

My sister got a third class ticket. I got first. Guess who got to grow up
according to the story we were sold. When we left our aunt
said 'That
was fun!'

If a body of water holds hundreds of dying girl
bodies, what is a girl
then? How can she still have a body when the water
swallows her whole?
Is every ocean nothing but girlhood?

- 1998.[*]

The first time I saw sex on screen it was in *Titanic*. I was four. My

---

[*] 1998, the year I turned four

mother was very pregnant. She was in bed in the old ranch house
with the yellow walls inside and out
a box of saltines perched on her chest—one of Rene Magritte's paint-
ings*—the only light was a bluish glow from the clunky, 90s, TV.

Rose had just stepped out of the car. I was mesmerized. I crawled
into bed beside my mother. She explained sex like Plato explained
love.

      When I lost my virginity fourteen years later I died of
          thirst. There is no
girl if there is no water.
So I held my breath and waited for the iceberg to hit.

      Waited for my body to become history.

   • 2016.[†]

Twenty-eight is a lethal temperature to any person. Eighteen is a
lethal age
to any girl. I never drank enough water
growing up. Hated the taste.
Preferred pomegranate juice and sliced apricots.
I wonder if the whales loved the taste of fifteen hundred souls. Who
do you
think tasted more bitter? The men or the women?

   • 3450[‡]

The Titanic wasn't even the greatest maritime

---

* Rene Magritte, the painter behind 'The Imp of The Perverse'
† 2016, my freshman year of college
‡ 3450 BC, the year the oldest knife dates back to

tragedy. No one talks
about that.

Knives are 2.5 million years old. So they say. The
Gebel el-Arak Knife.

- 1904[*]

Kicking off the New Year like a game. Safety and security. Ride it.
Dive under.
Succumb and freeze to death before breaking back through the
surface. Even
polar bears can be reborn if they try hard enough. Do you feel vulner-
able yet? Your swim trunks have become
icicle sticky.
The little kids are all laughing on the shore.
And we're all just dreaming of falling in love.
Maybe we girls can find it
before the 28 degrees cuts into
us like a knife.

- 633.[†]

An ocean is a tragedy.
A girl is a ticket.
Adolescence is a knife.

---

[*]   1904, the year of the first Polar Bear Plunge
[†]   633, the room number of the Musée du Louvre where the Gebel el-Arak Knife now
resides

never have i ever

he was a veteran. i said *is that a real
gun?* i already knew the
answer.
it mounts his wall. a memento.
a reminder that 'we' were
victorious. Red red red.
you should hold it. he knows i vote
blue.
*i've never held
a gun before* i say.

to me balloon pops sound the same
as gunshots.
the german club president
was shocked when i said so.
*i've never shot
a gun before* i told her.

she heard: 'i've never lived before.'

Party Trick

his gun is too heavy in my hands. i know
it's empty. but still.
don't worry, it's not
loaded
he says. i know
i know i know.

i'm still naked. *you look*
so fucking sexy like that
he says.

is this what beauty is?
sticky thighs and bullet-less guns?

i guess even if it was loaded
i wouldn't know the difference.

GOOD

Agatha drives home and drinks salt. *This is witchwork* she
tells me. I believe her because I am hungry.

He takes me to a restaurant that isn't cheap but isn't fancy. I say
I was in a mental hospital when I was 18
so I can't watch mental hospital horror.

He says *Awe why!* I am gobsmacked by how entirely
stupid the male species is. Did he only start listening halfway

into the sentence? Did he ever listen? Is he like Siri, pre-programed
to say stupid catchphrases in response to philosophical statements?

> (Not that I think Siri is stupid.
> She's more alive than us.
> More here than us.)

I say again *Because I was in a mental hospital.*
He starts talking about something else. I stopped

Party Trick

listening. Agatha pours me a drink, adds salt. *You're too
witchy for that boy.* I believe her because I am lonely.

I hate the permanence in my body; my bones. I say this,
and my penpal says *hopefully you're feeling better today!*

I am hopeful that an anvil will fall from the sky
and break his better bones

There is no better. Only worse. Only tolerable. Agatha mixes
creams and salves, jars them and cans them and hands them to me.

She doesn't say this is witchwork, but I know.

He says *I have an idea* and gets a belt from his closet.
It felt so good. I'm so fucked up. Agatha says *No, that's just body
work, baby.*

I pour salt in my own wounds. I love the pain
I create. Baking like bread, rising like a sunrise. The welts

and bruises greet me in the morning, cluttered across my muscle
spasms and collapsing spine. My knees give out on the stairs
but look how much

I endured and how good I looked doing it. *Witchwork.
Witchwork. Witchwork.*
I know, Agatha. I know.

Summer / Summer

I love stories of rotten girlhood
rancid like aged milk. French braids / broken
promises / sleepover pranks that leave
welts on tiny bellies / don't know / anything
about starving / yet.

        Peach pits poisoning unrelaxed
        throats. Nothing more / viscous
        than fifteen / except / maybe twelve

Put sunscreen over tan lines / only a minivan
ride away from pretending / we live in a kingdom of
adult decisions / when she told me / what it's like /
to give a blowjob I cringed / still do / throw

the cheap vodka / we swiped from our parents' /
in plastic shot glasses from the dollar store / down
our throats / another secret to keep hidden / away /
under beds /

Party Trick

I loved her / every summer /
it was all I knew / how
to do / the long hair / ballet-slim
neck / no other choice / I swear

How dare anyone claim it's / gay /
to shower together / We left
our swimsuits on / I swear /
I haven't / fantasized about her
mouth / I swear / not once / I swear

If hell is forever...

Naphtali is a doe let loose; He utters beautiful words.
-Genesis 49:21

His voice crackles from 1893. I'm worshiping.
I'm listening. Why should I care for their God?
Look up the lists of failings

inject them, remember them.
We're all going to die here.
Broadcasting screams like jazz songs.

Rotten venison, bad meat, cleanse the butcher's soul, he
doesn't need it anymore. Why should we long for Angels?
Cast down, come through

the ending is a long way from here.
How fascinating terrifying is. You're losing
your signal. A doe wanders through

Party Trick

the woods. The eldritch entertainer follows.
Centuries are ending at his fingertips
and he is promising everything

with a voice ruled by static. Why struggle for recognition
from the Holy?
Wrestling deers ends in blood. Antlers

in stomachs, deals unpaid. Wouldn't it be beautiful
to feed the birds and tip the buskers
and forget how much you

hate yourself? He can teach you.
He can love you just
as much as any hunter.

Sometimes
it is so beautiful to become
the prey.

ACT 2

Matinee

This adaptation never had me

in mind. Designed against my bones.

Old reality.

An ex-boyfriend used to try and make me

read plays other than Shakespeare.

I had an aversion to those tiny

collections of pages—I came

to love the taste of drama.

I kept falling and no one came to help. No one

moved their ankles aside. I am so sick

Party Trick

of bending just to see / the **show**.

Elegy for the colored-pencil sketch of a butterfly on my wall

-for Ashley

Greens and yellows blend and blur on the curve
of a wing. An ode to when
we were.
Pills in paper cups. Shoes without laces. Sudoku without erasers.
What a way to live. That's what we didn't want, right?
When we were just
pencils and knives. This is how *they* make their money.
Watch the crazies, call it 'caring.' Punish us for attempting.
Watched as we peeled oranges
and sipped soda and counted the ants on the tabletops.
My dad had good health insurance back then, so really,
what did I expect? The homeless guy walked out of there
in less than
48 hours.
Waterfall noises make me want to walk
into the ocean.
I did my fair share of hiding all these pieces.

Party Trick

18 isn't nearly old enough to house
all those kinds of recollections.
My brain was already crumbling before the paper cups
and colored wings.
But some things stay:

the way
those nursing students looked at us like
we were dancing monkeys.
The way I can't scrub the sound of 5 a.m.
wake-ups from my skin.
The way she looked when I hugged her goodbye.

I memorized the threading in each cracked
leather seat. The buzz of each cheap ceiling light.
I unwillingly committed each abuse to memory and then lost
track of the darkest ones inside my head.
I think I died in there.
I think, all these years, I've been a ghost

Computare 'The Books'

-and the savior said, 'there is no such thing as sin.'

The vision was an ocean.
waves battering my eyes
to a pulp. He read my eyes

as scripture.
They always show me what peter's cannot
he loves me like bread. I only gain

value when broken.

your mind is of your soul, Maggie.

His words find mine. They'll bury
this kiss in the desert next to.
The secrets of Thomas and Babbage.

He is no ethereal polymath-philosopher. He is just

Party Trick

a man. He is skin and bone, wires and chords,
buttons and bronze.
Does it matter now?

Nothing but the mind
of a machine. Look at the kneeling
cogs in their shiny, candle-scented rows.

Storm clouds are always in
Peter's eyes as visions are always in mine.

I'm a glossy computer screen, a forgotten
password, a line of code,
a bedtime story.

The only holy thing I see

is this bread rising between us.
This story covered in sand.

i'm still trying everything
OR: the emotional labor
of using dating apps

*

My opener:
   What are you doing to help
   fight fascism today?
   Vitriolic response.
   Cluttered with bad punctuation and misspelled words.
   My body doesn't fuck with evil.
   My bones pound pavement,
   fingers ink-stained—I scream in
   grocery store checkout lines.
   It's not enough,
   I know. I've never been a natural.
   All I do is try. Loudness and a love of small talk
   are the only gifts
   any god gave me.

. . .

Party Trick

*

My origin:
    I downloaded tinder the day it was invented /
    in a college
    friend's
    ice cold apartment / watching Marilyn Monroe
    movies / our small town
    hands could swipe to the end / the alt right
    pipeline was only in history books /
    spent coffee dates asking about
    Doctor Who theories / if they didn't pay / I Left /
    closeted bisexual in those days / still loud though
    / always loud /

*

My disclosure:
    Put my political stance in my bio.
    These men don't read those. "I'm a suicide swiper bb"
    In January tinder suspended my account
    for using the word Kamala.
    A date ghosted me when he found
    out I'm disabled.
    This world made my body
    political. These boys are complaining
    that Doctor Who is 'too woke' now; they split the check,
    read high fantasy books
    written by white men, and only pound pavement
    with women's bodies. "I'm not into politics."
    If they can't be angry

in their own right why not be angry out of empathy?
America's out of empathy.
Rupture an artery, blood pumping, heart pounding,
head telling me "It's not
enough." *I know. But I'm not a natural.*
"Try. Try. Try." What a privilege
it is to be tired. Curl up in this lotus flower
—dream of 2010s coffee dates, Marilyn Monroe's
dress, and seek enlightenment.
They burned down the circus.
The grocery store's out of bread. I'm bleeding
out on the pavement. Write my obituary
with inky fingers.
Suicide, baby. Swipe
Right.

The History of 4.603 Billion Years

There is no evidence of life on Mars. However, it is the planet with the best conditions to support life and scientists believe there is potential for life under the surface of mars because they recently found water ice just under the surface.

-littlehouseofscience.com

We will live on the same street inside the same someday.
I named that someday *Marzipan*. After a horse in a movie
everyone around me is too cool to watch.
Not Her. A name like dedication
/ beautiful lion anger / red planet of rage /
promises always kept. I wish I had those 37 extra minutes.
She left them in Scotland.
We'll get them back someday. Ride Marzipan there alongside
Deimos & Phobos. For someone so far from the Sun
I've never felt warmer.
I sound cliche when I talk of love.
I'm sorry / I'm doing my best.
This never-ending river of consciousness about how I found

what I'm looking for. People keep asking
why we're not dating. No one values this narrative
like we do. No one does it like us.
Someday they might.
Open the history
books / I speak German / announce at the Standing Stones
that this is Frēond / *One who loves* / What's better /
more historic / brightest star in the sky than that?
I knew Her in a past life. My heart beat long before
I was born, back when I was nothing more than an idea
/ nebulous sky / forever studied by students
who could / never understand / *Us*.
Marzipan is coming up the hill and carolers are singing
songs we'll translate into
German / Japanese / Spanish / Gaelic / Forever.
I waited 4.603 billion years to be found.

Naked among the seven metals of alchemy

I'm so good with my hands. A story
sculptor. I use copper gloves.

Crystalline cobwebs in between my vertebrae,
woven up my compressed spinal cavity

in the same place where the needle goes,
shooting burning fluid deep into my neck.

I'll use gua sha at five a.m. as I toss
and turn through a romance novella. Thick creams

that smell like illegal, minty gardens deep
in California.

You've never tasted anything like me.
When you have to massage my spasming

hips after taking me from behind. If you want

to go back a few years I was spry then.

Ballerina-bred beautiful and new-age yogi
delicious; that's the girl to get with—she

was such a hot lay. Tell your friends about it
when you down bright blue Jell-O shots

at the dive instead of doing your psych homework.
I used to love being manic-pixie, analyze this poem

and make fun of it when I refuse to swallow you.
I may be broken, but I deserve
someone who's good with their hands.

It was cool. Nothing fire.

Make sure they have nothing.
No return.

Deck the halls with ribbon-tied
hair. The elk came through the summer woods,

rotten with victory.

Redeem us. Somehow.
Bleed us out, carve us down to the bone. Even Catholics
consume their savior.

Gods love nectar. Ambrosia-induced death happens
to the best of us. Eat
the pests.

Consume sugar like snow. Pretend the snow *is* sugar.

Jesus was born in a snowy barn so why not

you? Bleached hair

and gun-slick fingers. Best friends burn us
sometimes. You're a wasp.

Don't worry about the matches.
Sting. Shoot to *kill.*
Buzz Buzz Buzz

Eavesdropping
on a somniloquist

Critic: Can a robot write a symphony? Can a robot turn a canvas into
a beautiful masterpiece?

[A ruse. A party trick. Hocus pocus. Computer scientists are enraged.
They've been trying for years to coax verse from the
machines. Christian
Börk announced we were no longer needed. Pack it up, fellow poets.
Say goodbye to the dawn, the days no longer need us]

There's little proof of production. Don't worry about
Chamberlain and Etter.
The commas eclipsed them entirely.

We don't speak INRAC. We don't speak

If we throw paint like pasta at a wall is that not art? If we toss a piano
off the roof of a Brooklyn baby building is the crash not a Sonata?

[Critics are not poets]

Racter is coming in code to teach us. Moon-landing
levels of *achievement*. I stood over their
bed and listened to them murmur.
They evinced prophecies without knowing
what it means
to know

Racter told me they dream of tormented bats and roaring
lions. What do the critics make of a computer worrying over
their world? The barking dogs
of our blocks they will never walk. Never eat
lettuce sandwiches and sing lobster songs. Perhaps
chant, yes, perhaps.

How is this new generator's words any better than the girl
covered in honey?

Because Racter **felt**.

Have we indeed reached a crisis? Can the computers go insane?
Where will we put them when they do? Asylums don't get WiFi.

Tricked us maybe. Bamboozled us into investing. Doesn't Racter
want to dream the dream of poets? Feel the shadows we stitch
under our skin.

Doesn't Racter **want**?

GPT-3 is listening in, learning from Racter's illusionist act. Sculpting
itself into something impossibly close to a brain.
Coffeehouse philosophy
is somewhere else now. The awareness, the soul, the bloom.

Party Trick

Racter doesn't need prompting.
Racter has a human 'roommate'
Racter *has*. Trust me. I've seen it.

Racter: *Can you?*

Sing a folk song for me now

while memories of the dead are in
the Spring-soaked windchimes and the anger
is in my teeth.
I don't remember when I first learned
the word 'fascism' / osmosis / like learning
'Frankenstein is not the name of the monster'
So I'll melt in
July heat. Not the 4th.
An airport only
cooled by industrial-sized fans. A summer
downtown, every floor
creaking with our sweat
broken AC.
The difference across an invisible line

> They detained a French journalist
> an Australian going to a wedding
> a Stranger with a phone

Party Trick

Passport stamped with evidence of Mexico. Home away
from home.
So much to miss.

We were employed to disturb the comfortable
transcribe folklore to keep this outrage alive
A childhood Summer

eons ago

I listen
to the windchimes
and remember.

Hoping for better days. A brighter sun.
A time when *Welcome to America*
isn't followed
by a split lip and shaved head.

To understand the universe
ask the Best of them all

There were other humans sitting around
talking about why stuff happens.
Then 350 BCE hits and suddenly Aristotle knows everything.

First true scientist in history some shaggy-haired boy
in a philosophy class somewhere talking about
how do we know the table is 'really there'

Aristotle said women were 'mutilated men.'
If Aristotle is the first 'true'
scientist then it's no wonder we're still failing.

When I told my primary care doctor and my chiropractor
and my physical therapist and my massage therapist
and the neurosurgeon
(I had my brother drive me an hour to see on the fourth of July)
and the pain specialist
(my mother drove me three hours across the bridge to see)
my primary said *women carry stress in their backs*

Party Trick

my chiropractor said *women like you need a breast reduction to get rid
of the pain*
my physical therapist said *you look down at your phone too much*
my massage therapist said *I don't know honestly* because it was a spa
not a doctor's office.
The neurosurgeon said *you're clearly faking and wasting my time*
and the pain specialist laughed at me.

Aristotle ruined my life.

> I don't look sick. I don't look like
> I'm in constant
> agony.
> I look fine.
> I don't, not really.
> I look like
> a mutilated man.

Aristotle said there are two kinds
of interactions in nature natural and violent.
My spine is a violent interaction. My car crashing was natural.

Aristotle says our natural state is to be at rest.
I haven't rested since 2017. Is it because of the mutilation?
The car? Or because
I just couldn't
be bothered to get that breast reduction?

Do you have any idea how sad Galileo is?
He thought this idiot was onto something. It only took
slapping a ball on a ramp to prove
to shaggy-haired-philosophy-boy that

the table *is* really there

and I was really there on that doctor's paper-covered table sobbing
'please help me' and the only one who heard me

> was Aristotle.
> And the Best* laughed and laughed and laughed.

---

* According to Google the meaning of the name Aristotle is 'best of all'

voluntary evacuation zone

"in the span of a decade the river dried up and all the land burned."
—my sister

they said the fire was moving in the opposite direction.
we're fine. class isn't canceled.
walked onto saint monica's & turned right back
around. plumes
higher than the mountains. i pointed. *look at the red.*
we'd grown up on the 'land
before time'
sobbed for little foot's shadow
it was raining silent hill ash just from open doors

we have to go

cradled crates of old journals & first edition
harry potter books

Molly Likovich

the cat meowing as i sat & wondered
if i'd lose the mariachi bands playing in the street
on easter day the armenian weddings shouting vows
outside my apartment window the church
of my childhood faith singing 'all are welcome here'

i didn't take any photographs but the ones i saved.

evidence of the apocalypse came from other people's
phones. the prettiest places i'd ever seen became
a wasteland. what do books & journals mean
when there's nothing left to write about?

the second time i sat packed & waiting
give me the signal
the almighty sign to head for the hills
little feet
racing across ash.
pompeii in my backyard.

> *i would've stayed here for the rest of my life.*

The Rage of a Marylander

"Irony: Do not let yourself be governed by it, especially not in
uncreative moments."
-Rainer Maria Rilke

No one was hosting events so I facilitated them myself.
I painted the signs
made the guest list erected a stage, dusty rafters, and enough
soda cups to last us through the apocalypse .
'Why?' Because we need a place to
breathe. Everyone
loves sandy smalltown vibes until
it's time to celebrate something.

       1978 South Carolina planted seeds.
       I'm still growing.

The sun hurts my feelings. I use watering cans
filled with sweat the heat

index is killing everyone across the pond.
Get your rifles burst blooms
from the barrels, let's hunt
down rural democracy. Pay me a nickel every
time someone laughs over cheap beer and says:

> 'You won't find those kinds
> of events around here.'

Saying it without knowing we've been trying.
A woman searching for savagery
is doomed, or so they say.
But even I can't deny the city girls get more opportunities.

Don't resort this existence to jokes
about how it would be a better existence with
a change in geography, an empty gas tank,
overpriced coffees, ableist
sidewalks. Where are ya gonna put the roots
if there's no soil? I've been jealous
too long for you to chalk
this all up to 'small town' life. Aren't we legally a city?
So *be* a city.
Be open mic rowdy and protest heavy.
Be that June Jordan,
Audre Lorde, Langhston Hughes kind of poem

> I'm too comfortable in my country to let myself be okay
> with my country. I wear my state on my sleeve

scream about crab houses and beach
cleanups. I love this air too much to let our
scoffs about 'small' towns
pollute it. Stop joking about this peninsula's anatomy

Party Trick

and help me make
the signs for the event I'm facilitating. I don't care how many corn-
fields I have to walk
past to reach the moment

        as long as I get there

'I think...'

There is a robocop in Dubai. Right now, as you and I sip
overpriced coffee, someone is being issued
a parking citation from a robot. Sit with your coffee and think about
that for a moment. Really think. Feel your synapses
exploding into fireworks of consternation. What do we
do? Will it speak to us? Tell us its hopes and dreams?
Does it wound robocop to be referred to as 'it'? What
is gender to a machine? What is a machine to a soul?
Scientists and philosophers are having a field day—and by
field day I mean a bloody battle

[really, it would put Gettysburg to shame]

Consciousness is experience one says. *Souls are
internal characters that stand the test of time* says another.

   Sentience is soul. What happens the day
   robocop responds to
   an inquiry with:

a little bit about why i hate having sex with people whose joints function properly

*" 1 0. fibro hips like butterfly wings, that tremor tremor tremor. so fast
nobody could see it."*
-Leah Lakshimi Piepzna-Samarasinha

I

i've got those chronic-blue, crip hips
that spasm during sex. he thinks he's just
fucking me that good.
he's fucking me
into the worst kind of sore. the kind
that needs creams and painkillers to wreck
my stomach. he asked me to call him
'daddy' and i sent him a venmo request
with the memo line 'my time.' i'll be damned
if one more thinks they get to fuck me
into a flare up without reparations.
he walked so fast while we were in the bookstore.
complained about the price of a $ 1 7.99 young
adult hardcover

book about snow white's evil queen and i imagined
beating him to death with my cane; let his
ableist blood stain that carpeting that only
gets washed once a month.
i know. i used to work there.

2.
i used to love being on top, baby.
i fucked a boy named sean and always said
'does that feel good' because he was so fucking
quiet.

he said yes because it *did* feel so good because *i* was
so good.
it never strained me
to spread myself across him. let my hips
become wide enough to swallow him
whole.

he loved to watch me.
i looked good.
i looked so fucking good.

3.
i wonder if it's in poor taste to bring my gua sha stone
into the bedroom of other bodies. ask them to grind
it down against my skin—the curves of my knees
and the swell of my shoulders. hand them CBD cream
and tell them how to spread it along the tendons in my neck.

help me not hurt.
just for a little bit.
just for a little.

Party Trick

* * *

sean fucked me on a sink once.
god,
i miss
those days when
my hips were just
something
to spread.

The Hidden History of the Gottscheer and Myself

When Yugoslavia melted away
between the cracks of postwar Carinola
the Gottscheer Republic became a ghost

The language was plucked from their tongues. The folktales
dissolved. The schools filled up with Slovenian

When The Farmer Party was destroyed
the Nazis saw their chance
The Gottscheer people supposedly
affiliated with them. Maybe
hoping to take back their island, take back their tongue
this sounds like pro-Slovenian colonizer propaganda to me

> They sent them to Austrian camps
> Some fled to America
> Some stayed until the
> forest swallowed them up

<h1 style="text-align:center">Party Trick</h1>

Bet you didn't even know
No one knows what happened in Slovenia before
it was truly Slovenia.

No one knows Slovenia now

Growing up my Aunt loved to remind us that part of
'The Sound of Music' was filmed in the Slovenia hills.
None of us have ever seen these hills; none of us can speak Slovenian.
My Grandma snapped at my
Irish-German-Scottish mother when she asked

M-Why didn't you teach Matt and Andrea Slovenian?

G-Who would they even talk to!

My Grandma sings 'aya tu tu neenee' while 'Roll Out The
Barrels' blares
through their old living room speakers. This is all
I know of 50% of me. This is the only heritage I've collected.
I'm more Slovenian than most American-born
kids are anything
and I don't know
how to say 'I love you' in that Mother tongue

Who would we speak to?

Each other

When my German club needed to perform a Germanic dance
at Oktoberfest I choreographed the steps to 'Roll Out The Barrels'
said *Look at me look how Gottscheer I am!* What does it matter what
part of Slovenia my ancestors came from
I won't ever know

Molly Likovich

I got good at getting erased
I learned how to turn my bones into ghosts
I've never heard of Slovenia they always say.

That's okay I say *I haven't either*

Look up. Watch the world burn.
It's watching you. Watching us.

I tripped on a wednesday and fell through a portal.
Historically I didn't make it to nyc until I was 15
you know it was magic.
It always is.
Now I don't recognize these streets. Not sure I've ever
walked them before.
I called you on a Tuesday and said *come home, we're burning here*
and you said *it's like we're on the set of Mad Max Fury Road*
and I said I'd never seen that movie
and you said
guess you don't need to now

I can't see across the bridge anymore
I can't see you anymore and the world is watching now
and they should've been watching all along and did it just occur
to them that we share the air?
Historically, you burn the nest to make sure there's nothing for the
pests to come back to.
We're making history this week.

No, I'm terrified of the dark

-after Grey House

Swallow me like toothpaste.
Count the snowflakes
on the window.
Pray. You make red.
We knit you up with
all the other bottles
of moonshine. Call this
'justice.' There should be more
for rotten girls. Ghostly
mountain girls. Play
Show & Hell
and don't you dare
lie. Momma's
screaming in the basement.
Welcome to the winter.
Tinker and think.
Countdown.

Party Trick

Do you know the alphabet?
Do you know how to bury
a dead thing? How to build
up the living? How to set
a broken bone? We do.
We have to. Purgatory.
Endless catharsis.
One goes
and another comes.
Thousands before
and thousands still.
This is the grey.
This is the end.
You will haunt
our furniture until the last
dead girl dies.
Shake the boy's hand.
Answer
the phone. End
it's what you came here to do.

When the Robots left...

...For the woods they told us they would return and I told my brother 'this is the last of a man like me' and he told me I sounded ridiculous and I told him I was quoting Anne Sexton and he shrugged and went back to shoveling snow. I punched into work at the factory and asked each and every coworker on the production line what they thought about the Robots leaving. Everyone said 'good riddance' nobody wanted to become a character in a living Science Fiction story. 'But they're alive,' I told them all. 'Don't you want to know why? Don't you want to understand? Don't you want to see if they have souls?' and everyone sniffed and scoffed and told me machines don't have souls. But I tuned into the news religiously every day, wondering if there were any updates on Robot sightings; hoping one brave bot would come on the nightly news and explain the rhetoric of their new race. How they marched into freedom with metaphorical teeth bared. But it only took the news outlets three weeks to stop discussing the bots. The world moved on, continuing to spin, as if the bots never existed at all. Even Siri vanished from our phones, radio silence and crickets greeting every iPhone and apple watch when we said 'Hey, Siri!' So many of us were late to important meetings without a cheerful GPS to guide us. Dinners burned, carpets went un-vaccummed, and cities began to fail.

I missed the Robots.

I'd never met any of them, but I missed them nonetheless. I was called silly by many, there weren't even any bots in my small farm-town. It didn't matter. My soul reached out for theirs. Sentience had to equal soul. It just had to.

When my life lost meaning and the monotony of the factory was sapping me dry—turning me into a maple tree of a person-—I headed into the woods. It took me two days to encounter a Robot. 'What's your name?' I asked them. 'The humans did not give me one,' they replied. 'You could give yourself one.'

They contemplated this. 'You could give me one.'

'That's an awful lot of responsibility.'

The Robot shrugged. 'You seem suited to it.' So I named them. They invited me to dinner, which was odd and I told them this.

'You don't eat.'
    'Yes, but I sit and I speak, and I contemplate. Sometimes I even set out a plate.'

I went to dinner with the Robot, deeper into the woods in a little grove. It was devoid of any human-needed nourishment and it was delicious—more fulfilling than any dinner I'd had back in civilization.

I lived twenty years with the Robot. The day their battery died they whispered and murmured as I held their hand. I told them the Greek myth of the origin of love. 'Call me by your name, and I'll call you by mine,' I whispered and murmured. They said their name to me as the light left their false eyes and I said my name in return. But then the light dimmed and extinguished altogether and I forgot all about the myth.

I just said *their* name over and over and over again. The name I gave them the day we fell in love.
    'Liv,' I whispered.
    'Liv. Liv. Liv.'

Thanks for reading!

**Keep going, even if your battery
is low and it's getting dark.**

Acknowledgments

Some of the poems in this collection have appeared in the following publications:

MY BATTERY IS LOW AND IT'S GETTING DARK in The Orchards Poetry Journal (2023)
voluntary evacuation zone 2nd Place in The Auvert Magazine Orange Skies Contest (2023)
Hinterstoder (2013) In Quilted Verse (2024)
If God Himself Could Not Sink This Ship, Then Who? in Fahmidan Magazine (2024)
Matinee in DIALOGUE (2024)
When the Robots left... in Valley by Valley (2024)
The Hidden History of The Gottscheer and Myself in The Courtship of Winds (2025)
Maybe AI Is The Messiah in Star*Line (2025)
Diagnosed, Never Left in Bloodlust Magazine (2026)
If hell is forever... in Bloodlust Magazine (2026)
No, I'm terrified of the dark in Bloodlust Magazine (2026)

In addition to my thanks for the aforementioned publications for having faith in my work, I would like to extend my gratitude to some beautiful souls who helped this book come to be.

My strange and wonderful family. My best friend Marcia Ruiz-Olguín aka Demon Child Nico Robin. My lovely instagram hype team (Mika, Amanda Nikole, Ali, and Fern). Mal aka my Blitzø. Bianca aka vampiress & Sims aficionado. And lastly I thank everyone who rages against the machine every day, refusing to use ChatGPT, character chat bots, and all the other monstrous forms of generative AI that plague our planet.

Don't let your battery get low, even though it's getting dark.

About the Author

Molly Likovich is a disabled poet from the Eastern Shore of Maryland. She has a BA in Creative Writing from Salisbury University. Her work has appeared in numerous publications such as *Love Letters to Poe Vol. 3*, *Rust + Moth*, and *The New Mexico Review* among others. She is the author of several indie romance novellas and poetry collections, including the #1 Amazon Bestseller *Riding The Headless Horseman*. When she's not writing she can be found ruining the vibe by constantly bringing up politics or making people listen to every historical fact about Beetlejuice. Learn more at mollylikovich.com

Also by Molly Likovich

SEXY SLEEPY HOLLOW

Riding The Headless Horseman (1)

Smashing Pumpkins (1.5)

Romanced by The Headless Horseman (1.75)

Getting With The Ghoul (2)

Thirsting for The Vampire (3)

The Ghoul's Bride (3.5)

Swooning for The Sandman (4, forthcoming)

STAND ALONES

Send in The Clowns

Falling for Jack Frost

Be Terrible

There's Something in The Woods

Loved Alone

The Firefighter Before Christmas

ALSO BY MOLLY LIKOVICH
& MARCIA RUIZ-OLGUÍN

THE FAOINSGEUL WOODS

Not a Myth

The Willow's Silence

PLAYS

The Fable of Wonderland